JOURNEY THROUGH

PENANG

a pictorial guide to the Pearl of the Orient

TIMES EDITIONS

Text and photographs by: H. Berbar
Editor: Patricia Ng
Designer: Jailani Basari
Production Co-ordinator: Nor Sidah Haron

© 2004 Marshall Cavendish International (Asia) Private Limited

Published by Times Editions — Marshall Cavendish
An imprint of Marshall Cavendish International (Asia) Private Limited
A member of Times Publishing Limited
Times Centre, 1 New Industrial Road, Singapore 536196
Tel: (65) 6213 9288   Fax: (65) 6285 4871
E-mail: te@tpl.com.sg
Online Bookstore: http://www.timesone.com.sg/te

Malaysian Office:
Federal Publications Sdn Berhad (General & Reference Publishing) (3024-D)
Times Subang
Lot 46, Persiaran Teknologi Subang
Subang Hi-Tech Industrial Park
Batu Tiga, 40000 Shah Alam
Selangor Darul Ehsan, Malaysia
Tel: (603) 5636 2191   Fax: (603) 5635 2706
E-mail: cchong@tpg.com.my

National Library Board Singapore Cataloguing in Publication Data
Berbar, Halim
Journey through Penang :— a pictorial guide to the pearl of the orient / —
[text and photographs by H. Berbar]. — Singapore :— Times Editions, c2004.
p. cm. — (Journey through)
ISBN : 981-232-595-6
1. Pinang — Social life and customs. 2. Pinang — Guidebooks.
I. Title. II. Series : Journey through
DS598.P5
959.51 — dc21   SLS2003037944

Printed in Singapore

contents

OVERVIEW

LEFT:
An overview of Georgetown, the heart of Penang island.

TOP:
The sun-kissed waters and golden beaches of Batu Ferringhi are a great incentive for anyone to relax and unwind.

ABOVE:
Two trishaws contribute to the old-world charm of the newly restored Cheong Fatt Tze Mansion.

The Pearl of the Orient

Penang state is located off the northwest coast of Peninsula Malaysia, is 24 km long by 12 km wide and has a total land area of 1,031 square km. It was originally known as Pulau Pinang (*Pulo Pinaom* in Portuguese) or the Isle of Betel-nut Palms in the early 15th century because of the early traders who came to trade in 'pinang' or areca nut.

The state comprises the island of Penang as well as the coastal strip on the mainland known as Seberang Prai (previously called Province Wellesley). The modern town of Seberang Prai has new townships as well as plans for industrial parks. Georgetown is on the island of Penang and remains the commercial centre and its cosmopolitan capital.

Penang beckons its visitors with a host of sights and tastes, and charms them with a magical combination of warm hospitality, priceless heritage, colourful festivals, and architectural delights.

Historical background

In 1786, Penang was established as a naval base and trading post for the British East India Company by Captain Francis Light. He acquired the island from Sultan Abdullah of Kedah who welcomed the British presence as it presented a challenge to Kedah's powerful neighbours. As the acquisition occurred on the Prince's birthday, Captain Light re-named Penang 'Prince of Wales Island'. A settlement eventually grew on the northwestern cape and was named Georgetown, after the reigning British monarch George III.

When Sultan Abdullah realised that the British would not render any protection, he gathered an army and attempted to remove the foreign power from the island. Unfortunately he failed and in 1791, agreed to allow the British to keep possession of Penang for an annual lease of 6,000 Spanish dollars.

In 1800, Penang's first Lieutenant-Governor, Sir George Leith secured a piece of land on the Malayan peninsula, just next to the island. He named it Province Wellesley, after the Governor of India at that time. This is the Seberang Prai of today.

In 1832, Penang, together with Malacca and Singapore, formed part of the Straits Settlements. It was well positioned between India, China and the Indonesian archipelago, and its port was a strategic base for the British against Dutch supremacy. Its importance declined with the rise of Singapore, but Penang soon recovered its fortunes by tapping into the tin and rubber trade.

By the 1930s, Penang was well known to the world. It had become the region's entertainment centre with cabarets, amusement parks and casinos.

During the Japanese Occupation from 1941 to 1945, Georgetown's streets and many of the buildings were razed during three weeks of bombing. The British had fled to Singapore and the people of Penang suffered severely during this time. When the Japanese surrendered to allied forces in 1945, reconstruction followed. Georgetown

Economy

As part of the Straits Settlements, Penang thrived as an entrepôt for the lucrative tea and opium trade between India and China. Trading was at an all-time high, with commodities like clove, nutmeg, sugar, coconut, pepper, areca nut, tea, cloth and other produce. Ships arrived from India, Burma, Indonesia, Singapore, and Europe. Penang was a liberal port and attracted Malays from Siam, Chinese from Manchuria, Indians, Acehnese, and even Straits Chinese from Malacca. The port in Georgetown was crammed with junks and steamers from Burma and Java, while more arrived bringing the Arabs, Sikhs, Madrassees and Klings. Georgetown soon became a melting pot of different cultures.

Penang's trade and importance declined as Singapore's increased as part of the Straits Settlements. However, this setback did not last long and in the latter half of the 19th century, the state's fortunes began to increase again as it grew rich on the tin mines of Perak. As the 20th century made its presence felt, the rubber trade in Penang was given a boost with a surge in demand for pneumatic tyres in the manufacture of motor cars. Today, Penang continues to be a dominant force in the country's economic landscape.

was given City status on 1st January 1957, and later that year, on 31st August, Penang together with the rest of the Federation of Malay States, became independent after more than a hundred years of British colonial rule.

Government and Political Structure

Malaysia is the only country in the world that practises a rotating monarch system. However, the monarch reigns but does not rule as the government is a constitutional democracy. A largely ceremonial role, the King or Yang di-Pertuan Agong is viewed as a symbol of national solidarity and defender of the Islamic faith. Once every five years, the ruling Sultans from each Malaysian state formally vote for one of their peers to represent them at a federal level as the next King. This began in 1957, with support from the Malaysian Government. The present King is the 12th and is the Sultan from Perlis state, Tuanku Syed Sirajuddin Jamalullail.

Unlike most of the States in Malaysia, Penang is not headed by a Sultan. (Other States without a Sultan are Malacca, Sabah and Sarawak.) Instead, the head of state is the Governor of Penang or Yang di-Pertua Negeri Pulau Pinang, who is appointed by the King. He, in turn, appoints the Chief Minister of the Legislative Council, the government body that advises the Governor in matters of legislation. The Executive Council is the state's administrative arm, assisted by the secretariat and government departments. It reports to the an elected Legislative Assembly.

Penang state has two municipalities, one for Penang Island itself and the other for Seberang Prai.

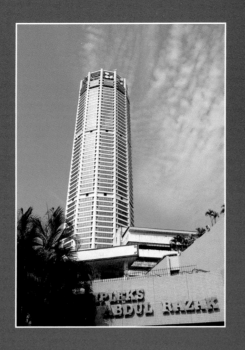

Architectural Milestones

Penang boasts of one of the longest bridges in the Asia and reputedly the third longest in the world. Spanning 13.5 km, the **Penang Bridge** links the two parts of Penang state, from Gelugor on the island to Seberang Prai on mainland Malaysia. About 8.4 km of the bridge is constructed over water, with 33 m rising above the water to allow for the passage of ships. This structural wonder, completed in three and a half years, was officially opened in 1985 by the Prime Minister of Malaysia, Dr Mahathir Mohamad. It is the only road link into Penang island. Road-users can pull off to the side at specially indicated places and catch a dramatic view of the harbour. The First International Penang Bridge Run was held in June 2003.

Komtar (Kompleks Tun Abdul Razak) is the largest and tallest commercial building in Penang, and the second highest in Malaysia. This 12-sided geometric structure has 65 storeys and is home to retail outlets, business establishments, government offices and a cineplex. For a breathtaking aerial view of the entire city, visit the Tower Viewing Gallery. On a clear day, the distant mountain of Gunung Jerai in Kedah can be sighted. For anyone wishing to take home a little bit of the island, a duty-free shop on the 57th floor offers great souvenirs from Penang. The Penang's Tourist Guides' Association is located on the third storey and is open from 10AM to 6PM every day.

ABOVE
Komtar is Penang's tallest commerical building from which you can get a spectacular view of the city. Weather permitting, visitors to its Tower Viewing Gallery can even catch a glimpse of mainland Malaysia.

THIS PAGE
The Penang Bridge is an architectural feat. Reputedly the third longest in the world, 8.4 km of the bridge is suspended above the water, rising to a majestic 33 m at its highest point.

PEOPLE &
LIFESTYLE

With a population of almost 1.4 million people, Penang is a peaceful potpourri of different ethnicities. This mix is mainly made up of Malays, Chinese, Indians, and Eurasians. About four per cent is made up of other races and non-Malaysian citizens.

Malays

The Malays or *bumiputras* (Malay for 'sons of the soil') comprise 52 per cent of Malaysia's population. Although they form the majority as a people, and have always held political power in the country, until today the Malays continue to rely on the government's New Economic Policy (NEP) to raise their status in Malaysia. The NEP gives Malays special privileges in almost every field including business, housing, and higher education.

In Penang, there are more than 537,000 Malays, making up about 40 per cent of population in the state. In the early days of Penang, most of the Malays who moved here were from the state of Kedah. They settled on the southern side of the island and created a Malay Town, making a living on agriculture and fishing, and being generally content with their rural lives. The Malays are Muslims and speak the official language of Bahasa Malaysia. Their culture is reflected in their ceremonies, lifestyle, artifacts, costumes and jewellery.

OPPOSITE
The commercial hub of Penang has lured people from different lands, including (*clockwise, from top left*) Pakistanis, Sikhs, Indians and Chinese.

LEFT
A Malay couple in traditional costume.

Indians

At the last census in 2000, Penang was home to 133,900 Indians. Historically, they had dominated the spice trade with Aceh, long before the arrival of the Chinese. When the Straits Settlements was formed, there was an increase in the demand for labour and this brought an influx of Indian migrants, predominantly from South India. They grew to a substantial number, as evident in the different types of temples built in Penang's urban areas. The Indians in Penang today participate actively in building the business community.

Eurasians

In 1786, the first Eurasians, mostly Portuguese Eurasians who had relocated from Phuket, arrived from Kuala Kedah at the invitation of Captain Francis Light. As they were better educated that most of the other settlers, Light felt that it would be advantageous to have them in government positions.

An enclave of Eurasians soon grew up around Bishop Street, China Street and Church Street (now known as Lebuh Gereja). Others stayed close to Farquhar Street where the Church of the Assumption had been built to mark the onset of the first Eurasians. More than 80 years ago, the Penang Eurasian Association was founded to preserve this community's unique culture. In 2000, there were 1,469 Eurasians in Penang.

TOP
These ladies, from an Indian (*left*) and Siamese (*right*) background, are part of the eclectic mix that is uniquely Penang.

MIDDLE
Indian barbers are a dying trade in this part of the world. They may not keep up with the latest styles but they offer inexpensive and efficient haircuts.

BOTTOM
Migrants from India often set up their own businesses selling everyday provisions to the local community.

OPPOSITE
The awe-inspiring entrance to the Khoo Kongsi Temple, where members of the Khoo clan gathered to pay respects to their ancestors.

Chinese New Year

This is celebrated at the start of the Chinese Lunar Year, which follows the cycle of the moon, and is auspicious for all Chinese, no matter which religion they belong to. On the eve, there is the traditional Reunion Dinner which is meant to bring families together. Celebrations last 15 days, during which Chinese invite their relatives and friends to their homes, and visit them in return. It is traditional to bring mandarin oranges when calling as these symbolise good luck. Children look forward to the *ang pow* or red packets of money that they receive from their elders. The more superstitious stress the importance of harmony in these 15 days and will not condone any quarrels or harsh words during this time, especially on the first day.

Chinese

The first Chinese who settled in Penang were mostly traders and merchants from the Guangdong and Fujian provinces in China. They arrived in the late 18th century, made the island their home and soon took local wives. Their descendants are called the Baba Nyonya or Straits Chinese.

Many more Chinese migrated in the mid-19th century and these consisted of labourers, coolies and artisans. Even so, the Straits-born Chinese remained a dominant force. They adopted a mainly western lifestyle but their womenfolk retained many elements of indigenous life. Their offspring were educated in the west, and they had a taste for the finer things in life. The Baba Nyonya of Penang, as opposed to the Baba Nyonya of Malacca, speak a Hokkien patois with Malay words.

OPPOSITE
In the past, it was not unusual for Chinese houses to paint mural-like drawings on their doors.

ABOVE, LEFT
A Chinese couple in traditional costume.

ABOVE, TOP RIGHT
A charming Nyonya lady in a traditional Baba outfit.

ABOVE, BOTTOM RIGHT
The Chinese word for 'dragon'. This intricately designed sign can be found above the entrance to the Khoo Kongsi Clan Temple.

Mooncake Festival

Also known as the Mid-Autumn Festival, this is celebrated on the 15th day of the eighth Lunar month. Originally, this coincided with the harvest festival but during the Soong Dynasty in China, it took on a political significance. During this time, secret messages calling upon the people of China to revolt were smuggled in these moon-shaped cakes with sweet filling. Local uprisings eventually led to the overthrow of the Mongols.

Today, mooncakes come in many forms, from baked to snow skins, sweet to savoury. Another tradition that has been carried down is the lighting of lanterns and allowing children to carry them through the village. Over time, these paper lanterns have evolved to include plastic, feathered and battery-operated ones. For this reason, this occasion is sometimes known as the Lantern Festival.

TOP LEFT
Weighing out the precise amounts of herbs in a Chinese medicinal hall.

TOP, RIGHT
Experienced fruit sellers can tell, by smelling, the taste of the durian flesh.

RIGHT
The Chinese consider fish auspicious as the Chinese word for prosperity sounds similar to that for fish.

OPPOSITE TOP
This trishaw puller takes forty winks in the middle of a long and tiring day.

OPPOSITE BOTTOM
The members of a traditional Chinese orchestra.

Hungry Ghost Festival

Chinese folklore has it that every seventh month of the Lunar Year, the gates of hell are opened to allow the ghosts to wander around. Many tend to be superstitious during this period as they believe that the wandering spirits are often up to mischief. During this month, traditional Chinese frown upon conducting any auspicious events like weddings and moving house, and caution youngsters against taking risks. Prayers, incense, paper money and food are offered to appease the ghosts, not just in the home but also in the community, where it is common to find Chinese street operas and other performances being staged.

LEFT
A Chinese opera performer in full regalia.

OPPOSITE
Paper effigies of opera performers (*bottom right*) are made up and later burnt (*top left*) to appease the spirits and bring good luck; Candles (*top middle and top right*)—colourful and elaborate—are also burnt as food for the spirits; The stage make-up for opera is an art form in itself and performers (*right middle and right bottom*) need quite some time to get ready before they are fit to face the audience.

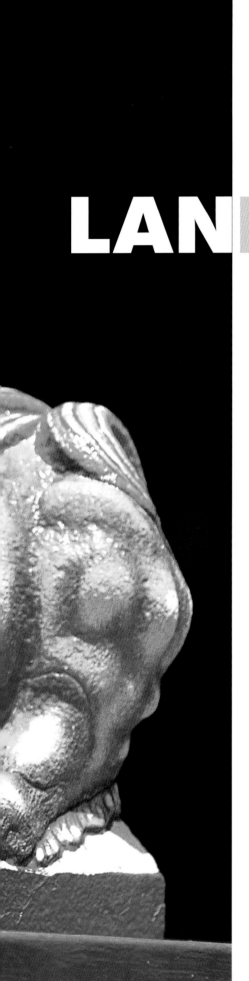

LANDMARKS
TO VISIT

OPPOSITE
To the Chinese, lions are auspicious creatures and it is not uncommon to find them at the many temples on the island. Often they are depicted in a playful stance, like this one found at the entrance of Kek Lok Si Temple.

ABOVE
The cannons at Fort Cornwallis have a long history, having been moved from one Sultanate to another. They were designed not just to be functional but also to be appreciated. Carvings found on the handles and parts of the barrel speak of a workmanship that is not easily found today.

Visitors to Penang will be amazed at the wealth of history and culture that can be found on this small island. Many of the landmarks are located within Georgetown.

Fort Cornwallis

Located on the northeastern part of Penang, Fort Cornwallis was built on the site where the British fleet, under Captain Francis Light, first landed in 1786. It was named after Charles Marquis Cornwallis, the Governor General of India, and designed to defend the harbour from attacks from pirates, Kedah and the French. Originally made of wood, the fort was reconstructed in stone, using convicts as labour, in 1808. Unfortunately, only the outer walls remain today.

Standing guard on the grounds are the cannons which the British had retrieved from pirates, who had stolen them from the Johor Sultanate. The most famous of these is the *Seri Rambai* cannon which was presented to the Sultan of Johor by the Dutch. Local legend has it that this cannon has powers to grant fertility wishes, and sometimes offerings of flowers can be found adorning its barrel.

In addition to an open-air theatre and public park, there is also a history gallery and handicraft centre. Visiting hours are from 8.30AM to 7PM daily.

Victoria Memorial Clock Tower

Standing at the corner of Lebuh Light and Lebuh Pantai is the moorish-style Clock Tower. It was presented to Penang state by local millionaire Cheah Chen Eok in 1897 to commemorate the Diamond Jubilee of Queen Victoria. For this reason, it towers 60 feet above the ground, with each foot representing every year of the Queen's reign.

The Esplanade

At the far end of the Esplanade is the Cenotaph, a memorial to the victims of World War I. Along the Esplanades' sea front is where the Town Hall and City Hall reside, next to the State Assembly and Court buildings. These impressive pieces of British architecture date as far back as the 1880s and feature spectacular Corinthian columns. The beautiful timber-panelled Council Chambers are still being used today.

OPPOSITE
The Victoria Memorial Clock was constructed in a Moorish style and is dedicated to the Victoria's 60 years as Queen of Britain. This was the brainchild of millionaire Cheah Chen Eok who wanted to give something back to the community that had helped him become a successful businessman.

ABOVE
The British built their government buildings along the waterfront and today, these are still used in a similar capacity for the local municipal governments. These buildings now overlook the Esplanade.

LEFT
The Cenotaph is a memorial dedicated to the victims of World War I.

Penang State Museum

Opened in 1965, the Museum showcases Penang's rich history and culture. It occupies only half the building as the eastern portion of the original struture was a victim of heavy bombing in World War II. A life-size bronze sculpture of Sir Francis Light graces the entrance to the building. It was cast in 1936 to commemorate the 150th anniversary of the founding of Penang and remains a memorial to its founder. The museum is open to from 9AM–5PM daily except on Fridays when it is closed for about two hours for Friday prayers. There is a small admission fee and the Museum can be contacted at Tel: (04) 261-3144.

Penang Heritage Trust

In operation since 1986 and working from its base at the Museum, the Trust strives to conserve Penang's heritage, promote Georgetown as a living heritage town, as well as promote the spread of information on Penang's historical heritage. It conducts a number of informative Heritage Trail Tours that trek through many parts of old Penang.

ABOVE
The façade of a 1930s Chinese house.

RIGHT
Captain Francis Light

OPPOSITE TOP
Inside the Penang Museum.

OPPOSITE BOTTOM
Part of the area under the purview of the Penang Heritage Trust.

Cheong Fatt Tze Mansion

More affectionately called the Blue Mansion, after its dazzling original indigo-blue exterior, the Mansion was awarded the coveted UNESCO Asia Pacific Heritage Award for Conservation in 2000. Cheong Fatt Tze was a highly successful businessman from China who was also the Consul General of China. As Penang was his operational base, he commissioned master craftsmen, imported directly from China, to build a 19th century architectural legacy that would reflect his status at that time.

In the 1990s, another group of master craftsmen were brought in to restore the dilapidated Mansion to its former glory. This 38-room mansion now serves as a boutique hotel and maintains a courtyard style layout with its original staircases, timber carvings, Gothic-style louvred windows, stained glass panels with art nouveau designs, Victorian wrought iron with Chinese lattice work, and archways carved with decorative dragons, phoenix, and flowers. The formal rooms are filled with 'feng shui' subtleties and portraits of ancestors grace the walls.

Tours are conducted and for more details, call (04) 262-0006.

ABOVE
These hand-drawn trishaws are the predecessors of the trishaws of today.

TOP
The Blue Mansion in all its glory.

MIDDLE & BOTTOM
There is a central courtyard from which all other areas can be accessed.

OPPOSITE
The spectacular detailed motifs of the Blue Mansion reflect the intricate and painstaking work that was done.

Khoo Kongsi Temple

Penang is a showcase of authentic southern Chinese architecture, and one of the most outstanding is the Khoo Kongsi Temple. Traditionally, a *kongsi* is a clan house for Chinese with the same surname or from the same clan. This temple was originally constructed by the ancestors of the Khoo Kongsi clan association whose forefathers came from the Sin Kang village of the Hai Cheng district in Xiamen, China. It was intended for members of the Leong San Tong (Dragon Mountain Hall), which explains why this charmingly quaint building has two portions: one for ancestor worship and the other for stage performances.

The Temple holds great historical and cultural value in the country. Built in 1905, this late Ching dynasty structure is a testament to the skills of the craftsmen from South China with its intricate carvings, hand-painted walls, dragon-emblazoned pillars, and richly ornamented beams. The Khoos were among the wealthiest Straits Chinese traders in early Penang and in the 19th century, they were very well organized and self-sufficient. The Temple is a reflection of the Khoo clan at the height of their prominence in Penang society.

This famous historic monument was one of the several sites in Penang where *Anna and the King* starring Jodie Foster and Chow Yun-fatt was filmed in early 1999. The Temple is open from 9AM to 5PM daily and there is an admission fee of RM5 per visitor.

This is a rare look inside the Temple as photographs are usually not allowed. The gilded statues and carvings, ornamented pillars and walls, together with the intricate roof, all reflect the wealth and prominence of the clan.

Armenian Street

This was also featured in the movie *Anna and the King* and used to depict the streets of old Bangkok. In Penang's early days, the Armenians were prominent traders, even though their numbers were small. By far, the most famous of the Armenians to emerge from this area is the Sarkies Brothers who set up the renowned Eastern & Oriental Hotel in Penang and subsequently the Raffles Hotel in Singapore.

By 1937, the last of the Armenians had left this area, During the mid-19th century, the Straits Chinese moved in, and they consolidated their position through clan buildings and temples. Once a secret society enclave, Armenian Street also served as a centre for revoluntionary activity in the early 20th century. It was the base for many supporters of Dr Sun Yat-Sen, the leader of the 1911 Revolution in China who later became the provisional president of China.

Syed Alatas Mansion

Situated at Lebuh Armenian, this is the former home of Syed Mohamed Alatas, a wealthy Arab pepper trader from Acheh. He was also the leader of the Red Flag secret society based in Lebuh Acheh until the 1890s and was instrumental in smuggling arms to the Achehnese resistance. Syed Alatas resided here with his first wife, a Malay of royal descent. His second wife was the daughter of a leading Straits Chinese merchant and leader of the Khoo clan.

From the 1930s, the mansion became the centre of a recycling industry headed by the Indian Chettiars. After World War II, the Municipal Council of Penang gained ownership of the site. In 1993, the mansion became the subject of a pilot restoration project financed by the state and municipal governments and headed by the famous conservation architect Didier Repellin. The Heritage Centre of Penang is located in the mansion.

ABOVE
Road-side stalls peddling a variety of tidbits can be found in Little India.

OPPOSITE TOP
Distributing the daily newspapers was a task that fell to the Indians who settled in Penang. Today, many still carry on this tradition. This man makes his base along Armenian Street.

OPPOSITE BOTTOM
At the wet market along Jalan Kuala Kangsar, it is possible to get fresh produce and meat. This may not seem hygienic, but for those who are particular about the taste of the food, this is one way to get fresh ingredients.

Little India

When migrants from India first came to Penang, most of them settled in the area bounded by Lebuh Pasar (Market Street), Lebuh Penang, Lebuh Chulia, and Lebuh Queen. Over time, this area—right up to Jalan Masjid Kapitan Keling—came to be known as Little India, overflowing with rows of shops filled to the brim with flowers, jewellery, spices, sundries, silverware, and silk sarees. This small section of Georgetown has become the home ground for traditional barbers, money changers, fruit sellers, goldsmiths, astrologers and other traders. Indian music blares from the shops while the fragrance of herbs and flowers fill the air. There is, undoubtedly, a nostalgic charm that sweeps over this little enclave.

Penang War Museum

This old military fortress, located in the southeastern area of Penang Island, was built in the 1930s by the British to protect the island from outside forces. Britsh Royal Engineers worked with the locals to create a fortress on what is

now known as Bukit Batu Muang. This structure, camouflaged by the jungle, was restored and converted into a museum to tell the story of Malaya during World War II. Visiting hours are from 9AM to 7PM.

Penang Cultural Centre

This is an ideal stop for anyone who enjoys guided tours. At the Centre, visitors will be treated to traditional dances, martial arts displays and handicraft demonstrations. Other attractions on this compound include a permanent exhibition on the Malaysian heritage, traditional games and other cultural highlights. Their opening hours are from 9.30AM to 5PM daily except on Fridays.

OPPOSITE TOP
This Muslim moneychanger has been a fixture for many years.

OPPOSITE BOTTOM
For a quick bite, approach these door-to-door vendors.

ABOVE
Snacks on wheels—this Indian man paddles his bicycle bringing tidbits and loaves of bread to the residents of the area.

RIGHT
Typical chick blinds that can be found fronting the shops in Little India.

Penang Hill

With a peak that rises 830 metres above sea level, Penang Hill is Malaysia's first hill station. The exhilarating view at its summit includes the skyline of Georgetown, the coast and Swettenham Pier. The perfect time to ascend to this cool retreat is at sunrise or sunset when visitors will be able to take in a breathtaking scene of the surroundings.

Amidst a beautiful garden full of diverse flora and fauna, birdwatchers will be able to appreciate the myriad species of feathered creatures at the aviary. The ridge at the top of Penang Hill flourishes with strawberries, a momento left behind by Captain Francis Light who missed the fruit so much he planted seedlings here. For this reason, Penang Hill is sometimes known as Strawberry Hill.

Visitors will not go hungry as there are restaurants at top of the hill, as is accommodation. The Bel Retiro, now a hotel within a colonial bungalow built in the 1800s, was once the residence of the last English governor. It was here that the flagstaff stood to signal its counterpart at Fort Cornwallis, giving Penang Hill its other name of Flagstaff Hill or Bukit Bendera.

The more energetic may choose to walk or hike up the hill, but this will take about three to four hours, with the most popular trails beginning near the Botanical Gardens. A quicker way would be to use the funicular railway, in operation since 1923. This is accessible from the Lower Tunnel Station at Jalan Air Terjun. The train runs every half hour and is normally filled to the brim, so visitors are advised to make their way to the station early. Each ride lasts about half an hour and passengers will be required to switch cars at the midpoint.

Dotting the landscape along the way are old colonial bungalows from the 1920s which were once home to planters, British administrators and rich Chinese. Tickets are at RM4 each and the train runs daily from 6AM to 9.30PM on weekdays and up until midnight on weekends. For information, call tel: (04) 829-9412.

Botanical Gardens

Created in 1884 by the British as a nursery for tropical plants, this 30-hectare garden lies at the foot of Penang Hill. A spectacular waterfall plunges to the earth from about a hundred metres up, giving this expansive place its nickname of Waterfall Gardens. Unfortunately this is now restricted to the public and permission must be obtained to view this wonderous sight.

The Gardens evoke a sense of tranquillity and are a favourite spot for joggers and picnickers. The long-tailed Macaque monkeys roam freely at this wildlife sanctuary but it is not wise to feed them or attract their attention. It is recommended that a walking stick or umbrella be brought along should some of the bolder ones decide to monkey around. Visiting hours are from 5AM to 8PM, and admission is free. Call for information at tel: (04) 227-0428.

OPPOSITE
The funicular train that runs the length of Penang Hill.

LEFT
Streams at the Botanical Gardens add to its serene atmosphere.

BELOW
The view from Penang Hill.

Tropical Fruit Farm

Situated 243.8 m above sea level, on the hills of Teluk Bahang, is the farm that was initiated to preserve rare and exotic fruits. Developed in 1993, the Farm was set up to educate people, local or foreign, on the legacy of the land and promote its rich heritage to all. The orchard, which covers 10 hectares, experiences a range of temperatures that best promote the cultivation of tropical and sub-tropical fruits, including the thorny durian—considered by many as the 'king of fruits' and a specialty of Penang—the exotic dragonfruit, the plump pomelo, the fleshy jackfruit, and the hairy rambutan.

At the farm, you can enjoy an excellent barbecue buffet with the family amidst friendly service, sip freshly squeezed fruit juices and savour all the delicious tropical fruits this region has to offer. For more information, contact Mr Quah Ewe Kheng of the farm at tel: (04) 229-3841 or (04) 866-5168.

Nature Trail

For those seeking to go on a *nature trail*, the Malaysian Nature Society provides trekking guides on the island. Most major hotels by the beach also organize morning jungle treks so it is advisable to check with the individual hotels for more information on these packages.

This platter of fruits consists of fruits that can be found at the Tropical Fruit Farm. Two of the more exotic fruits found on the Farm are the dragonfruit (*top*), and the durian (*above*) which has a pungent aroma that takes some getting used to.

Penang Butterfly Farm

Also located in Teluk Bahang is the world's first tropical live butterfly farm. With over 4,000 butterflies of 120 different species living here, the Farm is a paradise for spiders, lizards, frogs, water dragons and other tropical insects. Also found in the lush landscaped garden, which simulates the creatures' natural habitats, are artificial waterfalls, a rock garden, lily pond, and bubbling mud pool. The Farm is open from 9AM to 5PM, and the most ideal time to visit is when the butterflies are most active, in the late morning or early afternoon. For more information, call tel: (04) 885-1253.

Penang Bird Park

Located in Seberang Prai, the Park is only a five-minute drive from the Penang Bridge. It is a popular venue for bird lovers and bird watchers. This 2-hectare park is has a wide collection of birds, with over 300 species from around the world, all in their natural surroundings. While guests amble through the walk-in aviary, a variety of birds fly freely among the flora and fauna, giving them a first-hand experience of being in the wild.

The Bird Park is open daily from 9AM to 7PM, and there is an admission fee of RM10. Call tel: (04) 399-1899 for more details.

The Penang Bird Park is in Seberang Prai. It is home to more than 300 species of birds, some of which are allowed to fly free within a walk-in aviary.

HOUSES
OF WORSHIP

Over the years, Penang has become the new home of many migrants who came from various countries around the world. It is not surprising that different houses of worship have sprouted as a result.

Kapitan Keling Mosque

Constructed in 1801 by Caudeer Mohudeen, a merchant of Indian-Muslim descent, this is one of the oldest mosques in Penang. At the time, Mohudeen was Kapitan Keling (Captain of the Kelings) of the South Indian Community and the Mosque was named after him.

Initially the Mosque was a rectangular building with a slopping roof but over time, the structure has evolved to include yellow dome-shaped minarets and Islam-influenced Moorish architecture. Permission must be obtained prior to entering the mosque.

Acheen Street Mosque

The early Arab community flourished on Acheen Street. Here you will find the Acheen Street Mosque, better known as Masjid Melayu or Malay Mosque. This 1808 mosque was built on land donated by Syed Sheriff Tengku Hussain Aidid, a wealthy Arab merchant prince who came from an Achehnese royal family in neighboring Sumatra. Its Moorish octagonal minaret and other distincive features architecturally reflect the influence of the Chinese Muslims and Anglo-Indian settlers on early Islamic buildings in Asia.

State Mosque

Located on a 4.5 hectare compound near the junction of Jalan Air Itam and Jalan Masjid Negeri, the State Mosque is a fairly new landmark, having only been completed in 1980. Considered one of the most beautiful mosques in Malaysia, the State Mosque boasts of a modern design, with elegant gold onion-shaped domes and a chandeliered prayer hall that can hold up to 5,000 worshippers. Those wishing to visit the Mosque should ensure that they are properly attired.

The Acheen Street Mosque is sometimes known as Masjid Melayu or Malay Mosque. It has an octagonal minaret (*above*)—the tall tower with a balcony from which Muslims are summoned to prayer—and is Moorish in style.

Hari Raya Adilfitri

This is the an important festival for the Muslims. It is celebrated at the end of Ramadan, the fasting month, during which believers reflect and repent by refraining from committing sins as well as abstaining from food, drink and other temptations. It is hoped that by doing so, Muslims will emerge as better human beings and appreciate what they have and be more willing to help the less fortunate.

Muslims traditionally start off this festival at the local mosque with prayers. In the month that follows, they throw open their homes to friends—Muslims and non-Muslims alike—and feast heartily to commemorate the occasion.

Wat Chayamangkalaram

This Buddhist temple is home to the world's third largest reclining Buddha, a 33-metre-long statue draped in a gold-leafed saffron robe. Behind the statue are many urns which are said to contain the ashes of devotees. The Thai architecture of this Temple is unmistakable with its brilliant colours and elaborate designs. The Thais of Penang celebrate the Songkran and Loy Krathong, two traditional Buddhist festivals, at this temple. The Temple is located at Lorong Burmah and open until 5.30 every evening.

Dharmikarama Burmese Temple

Across from Wat Chayamangkalaram is Penang's first Buddhist temple. Its entrance is guarded by a pair of elephants and within temple grounds is a Bodhi tree and a wishing pond. For the Temple, the busiest time of the year would be on Wesak Day, which marks Buddha's birth, enlightenment and attainment of Nirvana. The Water Festival is also celebrated here.

Intricate designs have been carved into the facade and roofs (*left*) of the Dharmikarama Burmese Temple. Within, statues of Buddha line the passageway and fill the halls. (*opposite, top row*)

OPPOSITE BOTTOM
One of the few remaining snakes at the Snake Temple.

Snake Temple

The name itself may strike terror in the hearts of some but the Snake Temple is actually quite harmless. The Temple of the Azure Cloud, as it is also known, is dedicated to the deity Chor Soo Kong, who used to be a Buddhist priest with healing powers. Some stories say that during the construction of the Temple, a religious man who was transporting a statue of the deity from China, gave refuge to the snakes in the nearby forests. When the Temple was completed, the serpents remained. Regardless of how the snakes came to be there, the Temple became a sanctuary for poisonous pit-vipers who are believed to be servants of the deity. The Snake Temple once provoked awe and mystery when it was in its natural forest surroundings. Nowadays, there are few snakes left in the Temple.

Kek Lok Si Temple

This stunning structure, known also as the 'Temple of Supreme Bliss', is one of the largest Buddhist temples in Southeast Asia. On the grounds is the magnificent 'Pagoda of Ten Thousand Buddhas' sometimes referred to as the Pagoda of Rama VI) that rises 30 m above the ground, cutting a majestic figure on the hill at Air Itam. The imposing structure, that consists of seven tiers, blends architectural elements from Chinese, Burmese and Thai styles. Within this gigantic complex, you can find prayer halls, shrines, gardens, a turtle pond, food and souvenir stalls, and a striking statue of the Goddess of Mercy in the middle of the sprawling temple. The main construction was done between 1893 and 1905, but entire temple was only completed in 1930. Since then, due to the fund-raising efforts of the Straits Chinese, the temple has been refurbished, on an extensive scale, to what it is today.

Goddess of Mercy Temple

Along Jalan Masjid Kapitan Keling can be found the Goddess of Mercy Temple or Kuan Yin Teng, believed to be the oldest temple in Penang. Kuan Yin was a compassionate human being

who attained nirvana but chose to stay behind to help the less fortunate. For this reason, many believers visit the temple to ask for her assistance. Although this Taoist Temple is named primarily for Kuan Yin, it is also dedicated to Ma Chor Poh, another goddess of mercy, as well the Chinese patron saint for anything associated with sea travels.

The Goddess of Mercy Temple was constructed in 1800 by the early Hokkien and Cantonese settlers on the island. It is filled with intricately crafted details like pillars carved with entwined dragons. One characteristic feature of the Temple is in the inner chamber where the seated statue of a tranquil-looking 18-armed Kuan Yin can be found.

Devotees fill the temple on three major occasions. These coincide with the three anniversaries of Goddess Kuan Yin—the 19th day of the second, sixth and ninth lunar month. During this time, Chinese opera performances are held at the entrance of the temple.

Wesak Day

This marks Buddha's birth, enlightenment and attainment of nirvana and is the most important day for the Buddhist community. This feast falls on the 15th day of the fourth moon, following the Chinese Lunar Calendar. Devotees flock to the temples for day-long activities and at night, there is a street procession consisting of flags, flowers and floats.

OPPOSITE, TOP LEFT
The Kek Lok Si Temple rises 30 m above the ground and cuts an imposing figure on the horizon. Statues of Buddhist dieties (*top left and bottom left*) can found within its walls, filling devotees with a sense of calm. The pious visit the Temple and light candles (*above*) in supplication.

OPPOSITE, TOP MIDDLE
The Sleeping Buddha of Wat Chayamankalaram is the third largest in the world. Measuring 33 m in length, the statues' saffron robes are made from gold leaf.

Sri Mariamman Temple

The most striking attribute of this, the oldest Hindu temple in Penang, is its remarkable gopuram (the main gateway of temples) depicting a host of Hindu deities. Built in 1883, the temple lies in the heart of Little India. Its most prized possession is the priceless statue of Lord Subramaniam, embellished in gold, silver and emeralds, which sits on a silver chariot in a procession during Thaipusam. Visiting hours are limited from 8AM to12PM and 4PM to 9PM.

Nattukkotai Chettiar Temple

When the Chettiar community established themselves on Penang Street in 1854, they purchased land on Jalan Air Terjun (Waterfall Road) to set up a 'chettinar' or quarters. A temple was eventually erected within these grounds and this complex is still preserved until today. During Thaipusam every year, this temple is the destination of the silver chariot bearing Lord Subramaniam's statue from the Sri Mariamman Temple.

The gopuram of the Sri Mariamman Temple (*right*) depicts a host of Hindu dieties and this impressive display distinguishes it from the other Hindu temples in Penang. Within the temple, the walls and pillars are ornamented with more carvings (*right top and opposite*) of these dieties.

Deepavali

This is the most important festival for Hindus and commemorates the victorious triumph of good over evil and light over darkness. This is symbolized by the lighting of lamps at the entrance of homes and explains why Deepavali is also called the Festival of Lights. It is celebrated at the start of the seventh month of the Tamil Lunar Calendar and on this day, Hindus offer ritual food to deities and decorate the area in front of the main doors to their homes with a Rangoli, coloured rice traced in an attractive pattern.

Thaipusam

This festival is especially significant for Hindus from southern India and was introduced into Penang in the early 19th century. It is celebrated during the day of the full moon during the tenth month of the Tamil Lunar Year. According to ancient beliefs, Thaipusam marks the day that the goddes Parvathi bestowed the *vel* or lance on her son, Lord Subramaniam (who is also known as Murugan) in order that he could defeat and banish the evil demons who were plaguing the earth.

Today, many Hindus believe that this auspicious day denotes Lord Subramaniam's birthday. It is also viewed as a time of penance. Before the actual day, Hindus prepare themselves through prayers and bouts of fasting. During the festival, women bearing silver pots of milk and devotees carrying *kavadis* (ceremonial yoke) retrace the processional route that the chariot conveying the statue of Lord Subramaniam had taken the day before. They travel on foot from the Sri Mariamman Temple to the Nattukkottai Chettiar Temple, and finish at the Waterfall Hilltop Temple on Jalan Air Terjun.

Cathedral of the Assumption

It was in 1786 that Father Garnault founded the Assumption Church at Church Street to cater to the Catholic community, most of whom were the Portuguese Eurasians who had relocated from Phuket. Their arrival in Penang coincided with the eve of the Feast of the Assumption of the Blessed Virgin Mary, and the church was named to commemorate this.

In 1861, the Church moved into a new building on Lebuh Farquhar, after being in temporary quarters for four years. This soon became the focal point of the Catholic community, with the new building being able to accommodate 1,200 parish members.

In 1955, the Assumption Church became a Cathedral by decree of the Vatican. It is the proud owner of a beautiful 89-year-old English pipe organ.

St George Church

This is the oldest Anglican church in Southeast Asia, originally modelled after a church in Madras, India. Named for the patron saint of England, it was built in 1818 with the help of convict labour. The neo-classical architecture, of mainly Greek and Roman style, can be seen in the clean lines of the building and this has remained relatively unchanged over the years. A memorial to Captain Francis Light stands in the front of the church. There are services in English every Sunday. For information, call Tel: (04) 261-2739.

Christmas

Together with the rest of the world, this feast day is celebrated by the Christians on 25th December of every year. It marks the birth of Jesus Christ and is a time of sharing and giving. Christians from different denominations visit their respective churches to attend yuletide services which are sometimes preceded by pageants or short plays which recount the birth of Christ. Malls are often decorated with lights and ornaments to enhance this festive season.

OPPOSITE TOP
This Christian cemetery (*right*) has been in existence for centuries. The tomb of Captain Francis Light (*left*) can be found on its grounds.

LEFT TOP
St George Church is the oldest Anglican church in Southeast Asia and is home to a memorial for Captain Francis Light.

LEFT BOTTOM
The Cathedral of the Assumption was initially established by Father Garnault to cater to the Catholic Eurasians who had settled in Penang. In the Roman Catholic faith, the Feast of the Assumption refers to the time when Mary, the mother of Jesus Christ, was taken up to heaven. As such, a shrine dedicated to her (*opposite bottom*) can be found on the church grounds.

FOOD

In Penang, people are obsessed with food. The irony is that the best-loved Penang food is not that found in restaurants but that which can be found in the neighbourhood stalls or at the shop down the street. This is referred to as hawker food. In every nook and corner can be found a stall where someone is selling either some food, fruit, drink, dessert, snack or tidbit. More amazing are the hordes of customers waiting while the food is freshly cooked and served. With such a wide range of Malay, Nyonya, Chinese, Indian, and international food to choose from, it is no surprise that consumers are spoilt for choice.

Malay Cuisine

The main ingredients in most Malay cooking are coconut milk, chillies and *belacan* (dried shrimp paste). As with other Asian countries, rice is considered a staple food and curry is often found at every meal.

A popular dish with both the locals and tourists alike is **Nasi Lemak**. This is rice cooked in coconut milk that is eaten with fried *ikan bilis* (anchovies), *sambal* (fried chilli paste), and cucumber, all served on a banana leaf. Sometimes, the *ikan bilis* is fried with peanuts, and certain places include an omelette piece, peanuts or chicken as standard fare.

Another favourite is **Satay**, tantalizing morsels of marinated meat on wooden sticks, grilled over a charcoal flame and eaten with a spicy and thick peanut sauce. Satay is usually served with raw onions, cucumbers and *ketupat* (rice cakes boiled in a pouch woven from coconut leaves).

OPPOSITE
Satay, freshly grilled over a charcoal fire.

ABOVE
Ikan bakar (fish that has been barbecued on banana leaf) is normally eaten with a dash of lime, steamed white rice, *sambal* and a Malaysian speciality made of baby shrimps.

Nyonya Cuisine

Just as the Chinese migrants to Penang adopted aspects of Malay life and thus became known as the Straits Chinese, their food evolved in much the same way. Nyonya food is a combination of Chinese, Malay and Thai cuisine, and is quite different from the nyonya food from the state of Malacca. Some examples of Penang nyonya food would be *kari kapitan* (spicy thick curry), *kari perut ikan* (fish stomach curry), *asam prawn* (prawn cooked in tamarind) and *otak-otak* (fish prepared in a spicy coconut mixture and grilled).

Penang Laksa is probably the most popular nyonya dish. Rice noodles are immersed in a fish-based tamarind soup, garnished with sliced red chillies and cucumber, pineapple pieces and *bunga kantan* (ginger bud) shavings, then topped with a dollop of thick black fish paste. This combination gives the dish its unique sweet-sour-spicy taste which has won the tastebuds of many. A variation of the Penang Laksa is the Siam Laksa which has a coconut milk gravy instead. The best known hawker stall selling this local favourite is at Gurney Drive.

Chinese Cuisine

When it comes to Chinese food, variety is the key. The amazing diversity that exists in Penang ranges from Szechuan to Hokkien, Cantonese to Hainanese.

The most common Chinese food would be **Dim Sum**, which literally means 'a bit of the heart' but is used to refer to small portions of bite-sized food that are usually served for breakfast or lunch. Some standard items include *hargao* (steamed prawn dumpling), *siewmai* (steamed meat dumpling), spring rolls, *char siew bao* (steamed dumplings made of dough and filled with meat) and *chee cheong fun* (rectangular sheets of rice noodles rolled into a tube, usually filled with prawns or meat, which are steamed and served with light soy sauce). The best *dim sum* can be found at either of the coffee shops on Gurney Drive or on Chulia Street. However if you prefer to dine on these tasty morsels in a five-star establishment, head for the Penang Shangri-La Hotel.

Penang is well known for its **Char Koay Teow**, normally served for breakfast and lunch. In this tempting dish, *koay teow* (flat rice noodles) is fried with eggs, beansprouts, prawns, Chinese sausage, and cockles. Raw chilli paste is added to give it a spicy twist. For the best in town, try the stall at Lorong Selamat stall or Jalan MacAlister.

Another Penang specialty is **Steamboat**, where diners get to cook as they eat. A pot of boiling water on a mini stove is placed in the middle of the table and a wide selection of uncooked meats, seafood and vegetables will be made available. Condiments like chilli sauce and soy sauce are on hand to give the food more taste.

Bak Kut Teh (literally translated as pork bone tea) is a light stew made of pork ribs cooked in a Chinese herbal soup. This is usually eaten with steamed white rice or yam rice. Others

prefer to partake of this aromatic soup with *eu char koay* or fried yeast stick. Some of the best *bak kut teh* can be found at Gurney Drive.

Now available all year round, the **Bak Chang** was originally only eaten during the *Bak Chang* Festival celebrated in the fifth month of the Chinese Lunar Calendar to commemorate Qu Yuan. Legend has it that he was a scholar in ancient China who threw himself into a river when he was dismayed that the government of his homeland had been taken over by the Qin state. Moved by his patriotism, villagers threw dumplings into the river in a valiant effort to prevent the fishes from devouring his body. Today, the *bak chang* is a steamed glutinous rice dumpling stuffed with either beans or a combination of meat, mushrooms, dried prawns and salted eggs wrapped in bamboo leaves. While the Hokkiens use soy sauce in the *bak chang* giving it a dark appearance, the nyonyas do not and their version is white.

OPPOSITE, TOP LEFT
Char koay teow topped with prawns, squid, egg and beansprouts.

OPPOSITE MIDDLE
At a local drink stall, the juice from the sugarcane makes a refreshing drink in the humid Penang weather.

OPPOSITE BOTTOM
Poh piah is an Asian delicacy where a turnip-based filling is wrapped in a thin crepe-like white flour skin. The art of making this skin, as shown by this vendor, is a skill that is slowly dying out.

TOP
A range of roasted meats and poultry hang from the stall of a local hawker. This is often eaten with steamed white rice.

BOTTOM
Penang's famous laksa.

Indian Cuisine

Much of the Indian hawker food found in Penang comes from southern India. Rice is a staple and with a liberal dose of spices, many Indian dishes leave the palate numb from the combination of flavours.

One of the most popular Indian dishes in Penang is the famous **Banana Leaf Rice**—steamed white rice to be eaten with a variety of curried meats or seafood and cooked vegetables, all served on a banana leaf. To counter the spicy hot taste of the curries, a yoghurt-based concoction is often recommended. For the best the island has to offer, visit Passions of Kerala at Burma Square.

Another favourite is **Nasi Kandar** whose name is derived from the poles (*kandar*) that were carried on the shoulders of vendors who went from house to house in the olden days. Since then the vendors have come a long way. The poles have disappeared but the food has grown in popularity. It is similar to the banana leaf rice but is Indian Muslim in origin and the rice is eaten with an array of curried squid, prawn, fish or chicken. Lebuh Penang's Kayu Nasi Kandar is known to be one of the best.

Desserts

The desserts in Penang are truly delightful. One of the most popular is a cool concoction called **Ais Kacang**, which literally means iced beans. Fortunately this refreshing dessert is more than that. On a base of shaved ice flavoured by *gula melaka* (palm sugar) sauce and rose syrup is heaped a mixture of red beans, sweet corn, coloured jelly, *attap chee* (palm seed) and evaporated milk. In recent years, some stalls have offered the optional extra of adding a scoop of ice cream.

For a taste of the best, visit the stalls at Lorong Selamat and Lorong Swatow.

Another favourite is **Cendol**, which is a welcome cold dessert given Penang's sometimes sweltering heat. Like *ais kacang*, it begins with a base of shaved ice. This is drenched in coconut milk and *gula melaka* and topped off with green worm-like noodles made from green pea. Some vendors like to add red beans as a variation.

Nyonya desserts have found a place for themselves in the hearts of the locals and many visitors. These include *kuih talam* (double layered cake of coconut milk and *gula melaka*), *kuih koay see* (sweet rice cake), *kuih lapis* (steamed layer cake), *ondeh-ondeh* (coconut-coated gutinous rice balls).

To cool down in Penang's hot weather, try a dose of *ais kacang* (*opposite*), cold home-made barley (*top*) or this road-side orange concoction (*above left*).

For the best of Japanese cuisine, there is the **Kirishima Japanese Restaurant**. The restaurant's décor is as authentic as its food and patrons can choose to dine at the sushi counter, the main dining area or in private rooms.
Cititel Hotel Penang, 66 Jalan Penang; tel: (04) 370-0108.

The 1885 at the luxurious E&O Hotel is a fine dining restaurant that serves both classic as well as contemporary continental food. It has a relatively small seating capacity but carries an impressive wine list. It is closed on Tuesdays and opens only for dinner.
The E&O Hotel, 10 Lebuh Farquhar; tel: (04) 263-0630.

Other restaurants:
JAPANESE
WAKA
Tel: (04) 881-1811

THAI
CHILLI CORNER
Tel: (04) 226-2940

GOLDEN THAI
at Gurney Drive

CONTINENTAL
REVOLVING RESTAURANT
Tel: (04) 263-3161

SEAFOOD
ORIENTAL RESTAURANT
on MacAlister Road

WINE BAR
THIRTY TWO AT THE MANSION
Tel: (04) 262-2232

PUB & BISTRO
LEITH STREET
Tel: (04) 261-6301

Fine Dining

For exquisite French food, **The Brasserie** at the Shangri-La Hotel is first on the list. A choice buffet and a la carte menu is coupled with attentive and efficient service and set within an inviting, homely bistro-style interior. What this adds up to is a memorable dining experience. For a gourmet treat, there is the Table Surprise Lunch or Dinner where a choice of main courses is served together with unlimited servings of appetizers and desserts. The restaurant is open for lunch and dinner.
Level 2, Shangri-la Hotel, Jalan Magazine; tel: (04) 262-2622

Shang Palace at the Shangri-La Hotel serves superb authentic Cantonese food and specializes in traditional Hong Kong *dim sum*. With a seating capacity of 200, it is well equipped to cater festive banquets. Open for lunch and dinner, the Shang Palace, like most Chinese restaurants, is closed on Tuesdays.
Level 2, Shangri-la Hotel, Jalan Magazine; tel: (04) 262-2622.

At the **Feringgi Grill** of Shangri-La's Rasa Sayang Resort, one can always be assured of excellent Western fare, hospitable and friendly service and a warm yet elegant atmosphere. Patrons are always satisfied and are ever ready to sing praises of the restaurants many virtues. Not surprising that it is usually fully booked and reservations are recommended.

Ground Floor, Main Wing, Shangri-La's Rasa Sayang Resort, Batu Ferringhi Beach; tel: (04) 881-1811

To savour exceptional Italian food within a warm and cozy surrounding, make a beeline for **Peppino** at Shangri-La's Golden Sands Resort. Roving musicians who serenade diners give the restaurant a romantic air.
Lobby Level, Shangri-La's Golden Sands Resort, Batu Ferringhi Beach; tel: (04) 881-1911.

The best outdoor bistro is **Sigi's By the Sea** at Shangri-La's Golden Sands Resort. Here patrons can unwind by the balmy Batu Ferringhi beach, enjoy the magnificent sea view and dine under the stars. The bistro serves continental food to be complemented by exotic cocktails from the bar.
Beach Front, Shangri-La's Golden Sands Resort, Batu Ferringhi Beach; tel: (04) 881-1911.

Annalakshmi offers fine Indian vegetarian cuisine. The unique quality of this restaurant that has branches in four different countries is that all profits benefit the Temple of Fine Arts, a non-profit cultural organisation dedicated to the promotion of the arts. Also, most of the staff at the restaurant work there voluntarily. All food is served buffet style and patrons pay the amount that they feel the food is worth. The restaurant is open daily except on Monday.
Temple of Fine Arts, 1 Babington Avenue, off Barrack Road; tel: (04) 228-8575.

TOP
The dining area at the Lone Pine Hotel offers a serene and romantic ambience.

OPPOSITE TOP
Even though Penang is known for its hawker food, the state has many fine dining outlets which serve a select cuisine.

OPPOSITE BOTTOM
The Brasserie at the Shangri-La Hotel offers exquisite French food.

WHERE
TO STAY

Tourists may think that they need not have fanciful accommodations since they spend so much time sampling all that Penang has to offer. However, hotels are part of the Penang experience and visitors will not regret their decision to choose hotels that pamper their guests and make their stay an even more memorable one.

The perfect vacation getaway–relax and unwind in the peaceful atmosphere of Batu Ferringhi beach.

Shangri-La Hotel

Located in Georgetown's commercial hub, this hotel is only 20 minutes from the airport and at the centre of an impressive array of facilities, from recreational to business. It is within easy access of the historical and cultural landmarks of Penang, as well as many of its shopping centres.

The staff at this 440-room and suite hotel are well known for the meticulous attention they shower on guests. This has earned them the prestigious title of Best Services for a City Hotel awarded by the Tourism Board.

Guests of the hotel can be assured of the standard services and facilities like butler services, conference facilties, limousine services, spa and beauty salon, and a fitness centre. Golf enthusiasts will be pleased to know that there is a putting green within hotel grounds.

The hotel has a superb reputation for its food and beverage outlets, so whatever the culinary requirement, the hotel's tempting array of restaurants has something to satisfy everyone.

Obtain more information about the hotel at their website (*www.shangri-la.com*) or through the phone at Tel: (04) 262-2622.

Shangri-La's Rasa Sayang Resort

This is Penang's premier resort and was voted by Travel & Leisure Magazine as one of the top 500 Hotels and Resorts in the world.

The Resort has many Minangkabau-style features, most noticeably a roof that resembles the horns of a water buffalo. Guests hoping to get away from the hustle and bustle of life can look forward to relaxing on golden beaches surrounded by lush greenery or in the solitude of their rooms, each of which comes with a private balcony with a view of either the sea or the garden. Top of the line health and recreational facilities are available, including aromatherapy, aerobics, archery, horse riding and water sports. There are plenty of dining outlets serving a range of cuisines from local to continental to asian.

Interested parties can contact the hotel at Tel: (04) 881-1811 or obtain more information at the official website (*www.shangri-la.com*).

OPPOSITE, TOP LEFT
The Shangri-La Hotel has all the amenities guests would need to feel at home away from home.

CENTRE
The sprawling grounds of the luxurious Rasa Sayang Resort.

BELOW
While at the Rasa Sayang, try some recreational activities like putting on the green (*left*) and water polo (*right*).

BOTTOM
Outdoor dining areas at the Rasa Sayang will give your meals a rustic feel.

Shangri-La's Golden Sands Resort

This is another resort from the Shangri-La group of hotels and resorts and is often considered the jewel of Batu Ferringhi. Set in opulent surroundings on a prime stretch of beach, the resort offers all the modern amenities, not just in their spendidly furnished guestrooms and suites but also by way of their resort facilities. Culinary pleasures abound at each of its impeccable restaurants and exciting activities await the entire family.

More details about the resort can be obtained from their website (*www.shangri-la.com*) or through the phone at Tel: (04) 881-1911.

E&O (Eastern & Oriental) Hotel

Once known as the 'premier hotel east of the Suez', the E&O hotel has welcomed royalty, politicians, ministers, heads of state and celebrities such as Somerset Maugham, Noel Coward, Mary Pickford and Rudyard Kipling. Today, it is one of the region's finest grand hotels.

Full of old world charm, the E&O Hotel has Moorish minarets, a splendid lobby with its original dome and a 116-year-old Otis lift, all of which are beautifully preserved. Although the hotel only has 101 suites, most of them front the sea. Its elegance is captured within the old but beautiful timber floors, adorned by exquisitely woven Afghan carpets. The spacious suites are lavishly furnished with four-poster beds, the finest bedlinens and china. A twenty-four-hour butler service ensures that each guest is pampered.

Any guest who stays at the hotel will be able to partake of the timeless spendour that is the E&O. For more information, contact the hotel at Tel: (04) 263-0630.

OPPOSITE TOP
The Golden Sands Resort at night.

OPPOSITE BOTTOM
The E&O Hotel exudes an old-world charm.

LEFT
The various facilities of the prestigious E&O Hotel.

Lone Pine Hotel

In 1948, this was the first hotel to be established on Batu Ferringhi beach as the perfect place for expatriates to escape the blistering winter cold of their homelands in the west. After 55 years, the Lone Pine has managed to maintain its allure and recent refurbishments has helped it to compete with many newer and more modern hotels.

Located on a prime stretch of beach, the hotel boasts of beautifully landscaped gardens and peaceful idyllic surroundings. Secluded and highly exclusive, it can accommodate a maximum of 50 guests at any one time. Each cabbana-like room opens out to a private courtyard or terrace where guests can languish at their own leisure and appreciate the beauty of the seaside as the sun sets. On top of its excellent restaurants and recreational facilities, guests will be able to saddle up and ride along the beach or try out the various water sports that are available.

Find out more about the hotel at their website (*www.lonepinehotel.com*) and call them for reservations at Tel: (04) 881-1511/1512.

City Bayview Hotel

This cozy hotel stands in the heart of Georgetown, just a stone's throw away from the business and shopping districts as well as major historical and cultural sites. The hotel has a host of facilities but it is best known for its Revolving Restaurant, where patrons can enjoy a 360° panoramic view of Penang as they dine.

For a more detailed insight, check their website (*www.bayviewintl.com*) or contact one of the helpful staff at Tel: (04) 263-3161.

Stardust

This is a guesthouse with room rates as low as RM20. Located in the centre of Chulia Street, it offers clean rooms as well as a café and restaurant. Call the Stardust at Tel: (04) 263-5723.

Other Hotels

BAYVIEW BEACH RESORT
Tel: (04) 881-2123

BERJAYA GEORGETOWN HOTEL
Tel: (04) 227-7111

CASUARINA BEACH HOTEL
Tel: (04) 881-1711

CITITEL PENANG
Tel: (04) 370-1188

FERRINGHI BEACH HOTEL
Tel: (04) 890-5999

HOLIDAY INN
Tel: (04) 881-1601

HOTEL EQUATORIAL
Tel: (04) 643-8111

SANDY BAY PARADISE
Tel: (04) 899-9999

PARKROYAL
Tel: (04) 881-1133

SHERATON PENANG
Tel: (04) 226-7888

THE GURNEY RESORT HOTEL
& RESIDENCES
Tel: (04) 370-7000

THE NORTHAM ALL SUITE
Tel: (04) 370-1111

ABOVE
For an experience not to be missed, visit The Bungalow at Lone Pine, and enjoy a drink while watching the sunset on Batu Ferringhi beach.

The Lone Pine Hotel is so named because
of the pine trees found on its premises.
Sunset is a perfect time for riding
a horse along the beach.

Parasailing on Batu Ferringhi beach.

BELOW
Reflexology is the art of relieving stress through acupoints in the foot.

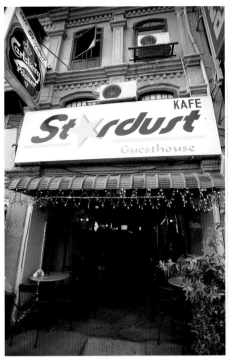

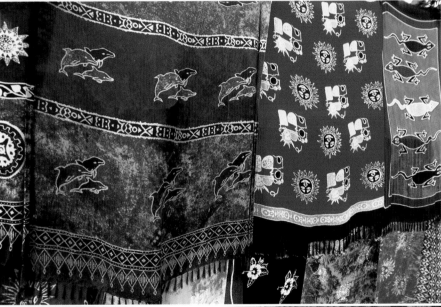

THINGS TO DO

Adventure At Sea

All the hotels along the beaches of Batu Ferringhi provide a host of water sports such as snorkeLling, scuba diving, sailing, windsurfing, and parasailing. Scenic trips to nearby islands can also be arranged.

The Malaysian Experience

After 6PM, the road along Batu Ferringhi transforms into a night bazaar where traders from all over the island sell their wares in makeshift stalls. This night market will provide visitors with a truly Malaysian experience, especially if they bargain for the best prices, as is the common practice.

City Pleasures

Penang also offers a wide range of entertainment, from discos to karaoke bars, from ballets to art galleries, from dramas to concerts. For information on the performing arts, check out venues such as the Amphitheater at Fort Cornwallis, Dewan Sri Pinang, the Geodesic Dome at Komtar or advertisements in the local papers.

TOP LEFT
The Stardust is a guesthouse with reasonable rates.

TOP RIGHT & LEFT MIDDLE
Walk along the beach and you will see a snake charmer and a display of sarong.

BOTTOM LEFT
Bargaining is common practice at the Batu Ferringhi night market.

ABOVE
For a thrill, try jet-skiing.

Take a leisurely stroll along the golden beaches of Penang and forget that the rest of the world exists.

NOTES FOR TRAVELLERS

How To Get There

By Air
The Penang International Airport in Bayan Lepas on the island allows Penang to be accessible by air. The airport is 20 km from Georgetown, about 45 minutes away. There are Malaysian Airlines flights plying between the country's capital, Kuala Lumpur, and Penang almost every hour, and Air Asia flies into the island three times a week. There are also daily flights into Penang from Singapore, Bangkok, Hong Kong and Taipei. Travellers should check with the national carriers on their current flight schedule.

By Rail
Although the railway line does not run into Penang island, it does stop at Butterworth in Seberang Prai and the station is within walking distance of the ferry terminal. The ride from Kuala Lumpur to Butterworth is six hours long but travellers will be able to admire the rural scenery from a comfortable, air-conditioned train. The KTM (Keretapo Tanah Melayu) operates the railway lines, and trains run from Singapore to Kuala Lumpur and then to Seberang Prai and all the way up to Thailand. For details, contact KTM at Tel: (04) 261-0290 or 331-2796.

By Ferry
A 24-hour ferry service links Penang island to the mainland. Return fares start at RM0.60 for adults, RM0.30 for children and RM7 for vehicles. Within walking distance of both the Butterworth Train Station and the Bus Terminal, the ferry plies the waters every half hour between 5AM to 2AM and every hour between 2AM and 5AM. From the ferry terminal on the island, there are bus and taxi services. For more details, call the Penang Ferry Service at Tel: (04) 310-2377

By Road
Penang island is linked to the mainland by the Penang Bridge. There is a bridge toll of RM7 per car. There are also bus and taxi services available at the ferry terminal in Butterworth.

By Bus
Buses are a fast and cheap way to reach Penang and they travel the length of the country from Singapore to Thailand. The best coaches are run by Nice or Plusliner bus services and they have up to six buses a day that do the Penang-Kuala Lumpur route. For more information on the schedules, call:
Nice – Tel: (04) 227-7370
Plusliner – Tel: (04) 323-1866 or log onto their website at www.plusliner.com

TOP
One option of getting to Penang island is by hopping into one of these bumboats.

ABOVE
The ferry that links the island to mainland Malaysia.

69

Getting Around

The city of Georgetown can be explored leisurely on foot or by trishaw. Alternatively there is the bus or taxi service. To visit sites on the rest of the island, it is more convenient to move around in taxis, but beware as most of them do not use a meter. Passengers should insist on a meter reading or agree on a price for the destination before boarding. Taxi fares to move around town are reasonably cheap. Flag down a taxi at any part of town or you can call the Taxi services at Tel: (04) 890-9918 / 642-5961 / 643-0161

Weather

The average temperature in Penang is a tropical 28–32°C with a humidity of about 90 per cent. Monsoon rains falls between September and December but the rainfall is distributed evenly throughout the year bringing the average to 255 cm.

Money

The Malaysian Ringgit (RM) is circulated in denominations of 1, 5, 10, 50, and 100. Due to currency controls introduced in 1998 and currently still in place, the ringgit is pegged at 3.80 to the US$1 and cannot be traded outside the country.

Licensed money changers are located at the airport, hotels, Komtar, Lebuh Pantai, Jalan Masjid Kapitan Keling and Batu Ferringhi. Most of them operate from 9AM to 6PM. Alternatively, currency and travellers cheques can be changed at all commercial banks during working hours from 9.30AM to 3PM on Mondays to Fridays. Most business establishments accept all the major credit cards.

Mass Media

Penang, as in other parts of Malaysia, has a 24-hour radio transmission with programming in all the major languages: Malay, English, Chinese and Indian. There are four local television stations—RTM1, RTM2, TV3 and NTV7. Cable television offers over 40 channels to select from, including CNN, BBC, and HBO. Newspapers are available in Malay, English and Chinese. The English dailies are *The Star*, *The New Straits Times* and *The Malay Mail*.

small businesses. Set in a colonial surrounding with luxurious foliage, wooden shutters and an eclectic mix of paintings, the Bookshop possesses an old-time ambience that makes reading and book-buying both leisurely and enjoyable. The shop carries a wide selection of books of various genres and specialises in Asian Interest titles and Malaysian writings. It conducts activities like poetry reading, musical evenings, book launches, talks, and plays, and children's story telling. Find more about the shop at its website (*www.bookshop-penang.com*) or feel free to call them at Tel: (04) 228-2252.

Best Places to Shop

For antiques

SYARIKAT PEKING ARTS & CRAFTS at Penang Road Tel: (04) 263-4334

LITTLE HERITAGE HOUSE at Penang Road Tel: (04) 262-6181

PENTIQUE GALLERY at Lebuh Chulia Tel: (04) 262-3028/2500

NYONYA HERITAGE at Armenian Street Tel: (04) 229-2203

LEAN GIAP TRADING at Chulia Street Tel: (04) 262-0520

MAG TRADITIONAL COLLECTIONS at Gurney Plaza Tel: (012) 409-2565

ORIENTAL ARTS & ANTIQUES at Chulia Street Tel: (04) 261-2748

For the best chick or wooden blinds

NGAI SUN at Chulia Street Tel: (04) 262-1933

For Chinese herbs and medicine or acupuncturist

KEDAI UBAT POH AUN TONG MEDICAL HALL at Campbell Street Tel: (04) 261-5825

For Books

THE BOOKSHOP is situated in Burmah Square, a heritage conservation project of the Penang Development Corporation where old government quarters have been restored for use by

Tour Information

Tour agents
Tour East
Tel: (04) 227-4522
Saber Holidays
Tel: (04) 881-1882 / 1678

For Tourist Information
Penang Tourist Centre
Tel: (04) 261-6663
Tourist Information Centre
Tel: (04) 261-4461

Medical Tourism

Over the years, new programs have been developed in the tourism industry. One such program is Medical Tourism where guests to the city are ensured the best medical treatment at any one of its eight private hospitals and have the opportunity to recover in a tropical paradise. One attraction is the reasonable price, due to the benefits of the exchange rate. Some of the medical services offered include plastic surgery, heart bypass, eye, and even brain surgery.

Events

Food and Fruit Fiesta
This is an opportunity for visitors to sample a little bit of everything—from local favourites like laksa to fusion food like Mexican satay. This annual festival is held along Gurney Drive and boasts of hundreds of stalls with participants from all over Malaysia. These include food manufacturers, fruit orchards, restaurants, hawkers, hotels

and individuals. This Fiesta draws thousands of tourists to Penang, all of whom are more than happy that part of the proceeds from certain organized events go to local charities.

Penang International Dragon Boat Festival

Dragon boat racing has long been a sport in China and is a test of speed, power and endurance. Although it was introduced into Malaysia in 1934, it only began its international journey in 1979. It became a state government project, supported by the Penang State Tourism Division, Penang State Water Authority and Tourism Malaysia. Its first race, almost 25 years ago, saw teams from Penang racing against each other

and two overseas teams from Asia. It has since grown into an international event with participants from Australia, China and Great Britain.

This two-day event, usually held in the middle of the year, features a 500 m course with six separate races. For its

25th anniversary, an extra race will be added featuring a 1000 m course. All races are currently held at the scenic Teluk Bahang Dam.

Malaysia Mega Sale Carnival

Shopaholics and bargain hunters will be thrilled with this event which runs three times a year, in March, August and December. The Carnival was launched to help the economic slowdown in the new millennium and has since taken off as a major event. During each month-long sale, retailers and other particating outlets offer major discounts, super bargains, freebies and special offers.

Shopping is readily available all over the city. The main shopping centres on the island are: Komtar in the heart of Georgetown, Island Plaza, Midlands One Stop, and Gurney Plaza. Other major areas for shopping are around Jalan Penang, Lebuh Campbell, Lebuh Kapitan Keling and Lebuh Chulia.

OPPOSITE TOP
For a relaxing holiday, check with your tour agents about your options.

OPPOSITE BOTTOM
The Food and Fruit Fiesta along Gurney Drive stretches as far as the eye can see (*left*). This is an excellent opportunity to experience hawker food in its element (*right*).

LEFT ABOVE
Dragon boats are so named mainly because a dragon is often carved into the bow of the boat.

LEFT
Durian lovers look forward to the Food and Fruit Fiesta as they will be able to feast on various types during a durian buffet.

Cultural

The ALLIANCE FRANCAISE is a non-profit organization founded in 1962 that organizes French language classes and supports the French Malaysian community living in Penang. Cultural events are organized to promote cultural ties between Malaysia and France. Its library is open to the public. Check their website for more information (*www.alliancefrancaise.org.my*) or call them at tel: (04) 227-6008 / 228-9719.

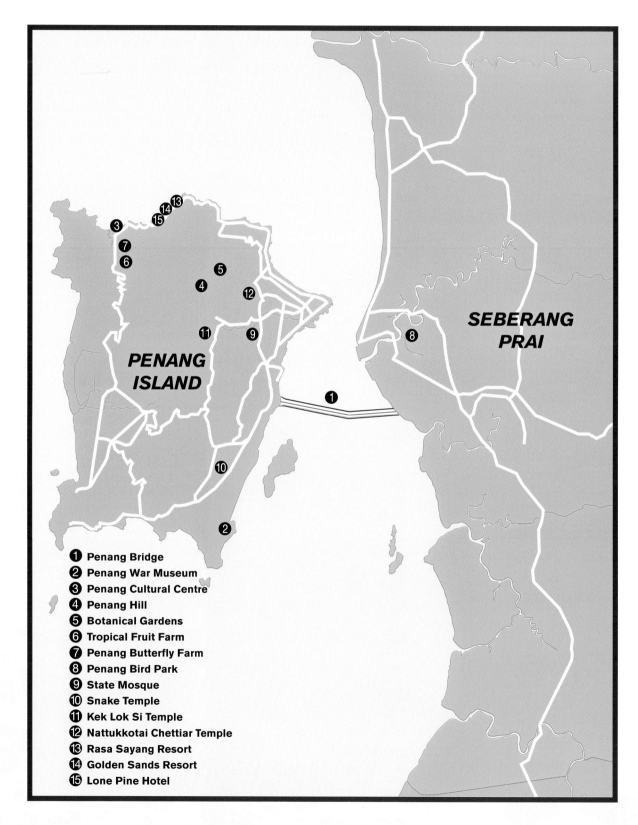

1 Penang Bridge
2 Penang War Museum
3 Penang Cultural Centre
4 Penang Hill
5 Botanical Gardens
6 Tropical Fruit Farm
7 Penang Butterfly Farm
8 Penang Bird Park
9 State Mosque
10 Snake Temple
11 Kek Lok Si Temple
12 Nattukkotai Chettiar Temple
13 Rasa Sayang Resort
14 Golden Sands Resort
15 Lone Pine Hotel

PENANG ISLAND

SEBERANG PRAI

THE STATE OF PENANG

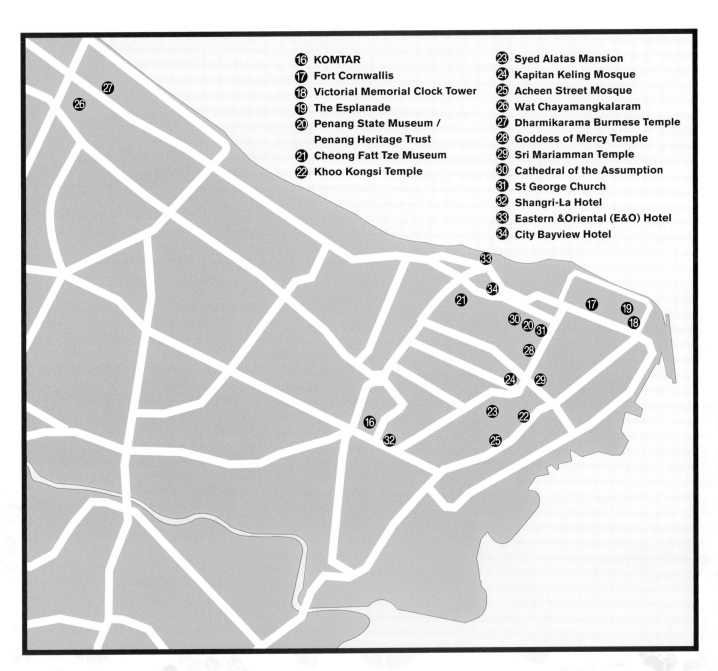

16 KOMTAR
17 Fort Cornwallis
18 Victorial Memorial Clock Tower
19 The Esplanade
20 Penang State Museum /
Penang Heritage Trust
21 Cheong Fatt Tze Museum
22 Khoo Kongsi Temple

23 Syed Alatas Mansion
24 Kapitan Keling Mosque
25 Acheen Street Mosque
26 Wat Chayamangkalaram
27 Dharmikarama Burmese Temple
28 Goddess of Mercy Temple
29 Sri Mariamman Temple
30 Cathedral of the Assumption
31 St George Church
32 Shangri-La Hotel
33 Eastern &Oriental (E&O) Hotel
34 City Bayview Hotel

THE CITY OF GEORGETOWN

TIMELINE

1786 Captain Francis Light acquires Penang island from the Sultan of Kedah in exchange for British protection; he officially takes possession on 11th August and renames it 'Prince of Wales Island'

1790 The Sultan of Kedah realises that the British will not help and attempts to move them off the island

1791 Kedah's attacks fail and the British gain possession of the island for an annual lease of 6,000 Spanish dollars

1794 Francis Light dies in Penang

1800 Sir George Leith, Penang's first Lieutenant Governor, secures a strip of land on the Malayan peninsula and names it Province Wellesley (now called Seberang Prai) after the Governor of India; Early Hokkien and Cantonese settlers build the Goddess of Mercy Temple

1801 Caudeer Mohudeen constructs the Kapitan Keling Mosque

1804 Penang elevated to the status of a Presidency

1805 The new Governor arrives, accompanied by his staff, which includes Thomas Stamford Raffles

1808 Acheen Street Mosque is built

1818 Convicts help to build St George Church

1819 Raffles founded Singapore and attention is turned away from Penang

1824 Malacca was acquired

1826 Penang, Malacca and Singapore were incorporated to form the Straits Settlements with Penang as its capital

1835 The capital of the Straits Settlements is transferred to Singapore

1848 Discovery of tin deposits in Perak on the Malayan peninsula, south of Penang, stimulates the tin trade on the island

1867 Colonial Office was set up in Singapore and the control of the Straits Settlements is transferred from India to Singapore; Penang, Malacca and Singapore become British Crown Colonies

1874 The Pangkor Treaty of 1874 signed and Penang flourishes as an export centre for the British

1883 Sri Mariamman Temple is set up

1884 The Botanical Gardens are created

1905 Penang is the first of the Malayan states to get electricity when the hydroelectric scheme is completed on the island

1906 The island's first electrical tramway is established

1910 In the West, motorcars become more popular and this spurs an increase in demand for rubber that is traded through Penang

1914 With the outbreak of World War I, Penang and the rest of Malaya prosper from additional demand for rubber and tin during the war years

1923	Penang Hill's funicular railway is completed and lauded as an engineering feat
1929	Wall Street crashes and signals the start of the Great Depression, sending Penang's economy spiralling downwards
1935	The island begins a slow economic recovery
1941	The Japanese invade Malaya on the 8th December; Penang is bombed
1942 –1945	Malaya is occupied by the Japanese
1945	The Japanese surrender to the allied forces and Malaya is reoccupied by the British
1946	Penang and Malacca become part of the Malayan Union
1948	Penang becomes part of the Federation of Malay States; Malayan Communist Party (MCA) organize communist uprisings and a struggle for power begins between the democratic forces of Malaya and Britain and communist insurgents; a state of Emergency is called
1955	The Assumption Church established by Father Garnault is 1786 is decreed a Cathedral
1957	The Federation of Malay States achieves independence on 31st August
1963	Malaysia is formed from the Federation of Malay States, Sabah, Sarawak, and Singapore
1965	Singapore breaks away from Malaysia and claims independence
1966	The first Malaysian Development Plan is launched with the aim of achieving self-sufficiency in staples and increasing the produclion of major export crops
1971	Malaysian government introduces New Economic Policy (NEP) to raise the status of Malays in the country
1979	Dragon boat racing becomes a state government project and the Penang International Dragon Boat Festival has its humble beginnings
1981	Dr Mahathir Mohamad takes over as Malaysia's Prime Minister
1985	Penang Bridge is officially opened by Prime Minister of Malaysia and Komtar is completed
1986	Penang Heritage Trust begins operations
1993	The Tropical Fruit Farm is developed
1999	Filming of *Anna and the King* takes place along Armenian Street and on the grounds of the Khoo Kongsi Temple
2000	Cheong Fatt Tze Mansion awarded the UNESCO Asia Pacific Heritage Award for Conservation
2003	Inauguration of First International Penang Bridge Run

DO'S AND DONT'S

There are several rules of etiquette that visitors to Penang should take note of:

- If you are a man, do not attempt to shake hands with a Malay woman unless she initiates the greeting. Similarly, if you are a woman, do not be offended if a Malay man refuses to shake your hand.
- Do not point with the forefinger as this is considered very rude. Either use your thumb or your whole hand.
- It is impolite to point your feet in someone's direction when you are seated. It is also usually considered rude to cross your legs, especially for women.
- It is offensive to wear shoes into a home so take your shoes off before going into someone's house.
- It is customary for a host to offer food and drink. It is courteous to accept this hospitality graciously.
- It is polite to wait for your host to start eating before you do.
- It is impolite to eat with your left hand or leave chopsticks standing in a bowl of rice.
- Shoes should be taken off before entering any places of worship and loose clothing that cover the arms and legs may be required. If in doubt, dress conservatively.
- Topless bathing is illegal on the beaches.
- Smoking is now prohibited in most public places, including air-conditioned restaurants, shopping centres, buses, taxis and cinemas.

WEB SITES

Cheong Fatt Tze Mansion
http://www.cheongfatttzemansion.com
Discover Penang
http://www.pulaupinang.com
International Penang Bridge Run
http://www.emedia.com.my/PBR/ipbr2003
Official Website of Tourism Penang
http://www.exoticpenang.com.my
Penang Butterfly Farm
http://www.butterfly-insect.com
Penang Development Council
http//www.pdc.gov.my
Penang Heritage Trust
http://www.pht.org.my
Penang International Cultural Carnival
http://www.picca.com.my
The Penang Story
http://www.penangstory.net
The Star Online
http://thestar.com.my
Tourism Malaysia
http://www.tourism.gov.my

ABOUT THE AUTHOR

H Berbar is a native of Paris, where he studied photography
before working with leading press and photography agencies in France.
Berbar has travelled extensively throughout Asia, Europe, Africa and
South America and has more than 25 years' experience as a photojournalist.
A prize-winning photographer, his clients include international publishers
and established corporations. Berbar is currently based in Kuala Lumpur,
Malaysia, and has been living there for the last ten years. He is also the author of
two other books in the *Journey Through* series—*Kuala Lumpur* and *Malacca*—
and his work can be viewed in *Orang Asli and their Wood Art*.

SPECIAL THANKS The author would like to thank the following for their contribution and generous assistance. ■ Dato Kee Phaik Cheen, Penang State Executive Councillor for Tourism, Culture, the Arts & Women's Development and Chairman of Penang Tourism Action Council ■ Goh Mah Loon of the Penang Tourism Office ■ Salehhudin Md. Salleh, Director of the Penang State Culture & Arts Office ■ Yusof Halmi, Director of Pejabat Kebudayaan & Kesenian Pulau Pinang ■ Shangri-La Hotel Penang ■ Gilbert Jung, General Manager of the Shangri-La Hotel ■ Tan Ti Ne, Communications Manager of the Shangri-La Hotel ■ Saw Wei Wei, Communications Executive of the Shangri-La Hotel ■ Gael Moureau, Executive Chef of the Shangri-La Hotel ■ Rasa Sayang Resort, Penang ■ Arbind K Shrestha, General Manager of the Rasa Sayang Resort ■ Suleiman Tunku Abdul Rahman, Director of Communications of the Rasa Sayang Resort ■ Eileen Chong, Communications Co-ordinator of the Rasa Sayang Resort ■ Eastern and Oriental Hotel ■ Adrian Brown, General Manager of the Eastern and Oriental Hotel ■ Ann Sheila John, Communications Manager of the Eastern and Oriental Hotel ■ City Bayview Hotel, Penang ■ Dr Choong Sin Poey, President of the Penang Heritage Trust ■ C. S. Cheah of the Trustee of Leong San Tong Khoo Kongsi of Penang ■ The Temple of Fine Arts ■ Michael Cheah of Nyonya Heritage of Penang ■ Ooi Bok Kim, Architect with APAM ■ Vincent from Stardust ■ Jin H. Li from Penang Tourism Action Council ■ Lee Wei Yen, HBL Network Photo Agency